Two Billion Dollars in Nickels
Reflections on the Entrepreneurial Life

by Kinko's Founder Paul Orfalea
with Dean Zatkowsky

Notice:

Although the authors have made every effort to ensure the accuracy and completeness of information contained in this book, we assume no responsibility for errors, inaccuracies, omissions, or any inconsistencies herein. In offering our opinions on leadership, management, and business in general, we intend no harm or offense to any individual or organization and hope none is taken. All trademarks used are property of their respective owners.

Table of Contents

Foreword
By Dean Zatkowsky

Sometime in the late 1980s, I took my father to the Huntington Beach, California, Kinko's to get some passport photos. We got the photos, and while the store manager and I discussed some ads he wanted me to design, my dad stood back and watched the cash register for a while. Later, Dad told me there was never a long line, but the cash register was in constant use. "You guys are making big money, a nickel at a time." Yup. By the time founder Paul Orfalea left Kinko's in 2000, the company was doing almost $2 billion in sales. That's a lot of nickels.

I've been working on writing projects with Paul since 1986, when I joined Kinko's Service Corporation as an advertising copywriter. Coworker development was a big deal at Kinko's, so along the way I read a lot of business books. And I mean *a lot of business books*.

I enjoyed books like Jim Collins' *Good to Great* (Collins Business, 2001), which I consider the best business book ever, and shorter books like Ken Blanchard's *Gung Ho* (William Morrow, 1997). I liked USC president Steven Sample's *The Contrarian's Guide to Leadership* (Jossey-Bass, 2002), and I keep a large collection of Peter Drucker's works as a reference library — there's something useful on every page!

Over the last few years, however, I've enjoyed business books less. Or more accurately, I've enjoyed less of business books. Traditional publishers urge authors to produce ever-higher page counts because bigger books command higher retail prices while economies of scale reduce per-piece production costs. Thick books are more profitable. That's why so many recent business books contain twenty or thirty pages of interesting ideas supported by three-hundred-plus pages of ponderous and often redundant examples.

Paul and I can't work that way.

On my first day at Kinko's, I was warned that Paul did not like to read, and I should never present him with anything longer than one page – and it better be in large type. I didn't know he was dyslexic, but I thought, "Whatever, he's the boss."

That one-page limit turned out to be the best training an aspiring writer could hope for. My job was to distill the key messages to the simplest language possible – no matter how complex the subject. Any success I've achieved as a writer is a direct result of that challenge.

I'm not a lazy reader, and I don't think you are either. But we are busy people, and we have our own priorities. I'll gladly spend many hours reading a novel, but I also have articles to write, photos to create, meetings to endure, kids to play with, and a wife whose company I enjoy. My to-do list does not include studying a business book's twenty pages of intricate charts and graphs that illustrate a concept I understood after one good example. Maybe I'm just losing patience as I get older, but I'm drawn to slimmer business books these days because I expect people to just get to the point. And maybe it's the Kinkoid toner in my blood, but wasted paper drives me crazy.

Thanks to the BookSurge print-on-demand publishing service, which I consider a descendant of Kinko's mid-1980s Custom Publishing product, Paul and I don't have to pad our books with extra pages just to pad our publisher's pockets. We don't have to waste paper, ink, and fossil fuels. Paul has always said that *inventory* is the dirtiest word in business for both cash flow and waste reasons. Thanks to print-on-demand, the book in your hands is truly your copy – it was made just for you. It's a thin book, but we hope you'll find a useful idea on each page. We've kept the price low so that even if you only find a useful idea on every fifth page, the book should still be a good value.

I've learned a lot from Paul Orfalea over the last twenty-two years, but here is the most important thing he has taught me: *Entrepreneurship is not about owning a business; it's about owning your life.* His entrepreneurial philosophy melds business, personal finances, lifelong learning, and the pursuit of happiness. It's a very uplifting and rewarding way of looking at the world.

Here, then, is a small collection of essays and questions for entrepreneurs and people who want to live more entrepreneurially. Portions of this book were published previously on Paul's Web site (www.paulorfalea.com) or in our *Tolosa Press* (www.tolosapress. com) newspaper columns. A version of Paul's introduction appeared in the International Dyslexia Association's quarterly journal, *Perspectives*. You can read this thin volume quickly, but we hope you'll be pondering its ideas and questions for a long time to come. Some of these concepts will be covered in more depth in our forthcoming book, *Kamelot: Kinko's Brief Shining Moment in Business History*. In the meantime, we hope you enjoy and profit from these bite-sized nuggets of Paul's entrepreneurial wisdom.

Introduction: An Eye for Opportunity
By Paul Orfalea

All Kinds of Minds cofounder and University of North Carolina at Chapel Hill professor of pediatrics Dr. Mel Levine says, "Teachers must realize that the very qualities that trip up a child may be the source of his success as an adult." That was sure true in my case. I couldn't read, and I couldn't sit still. These are not great traits for most students, but what blessings they turned out to be for me!

Dyslexia and hyperactivity make school difficult today, but imagine how difficult it was in the early 1950s – in Catholic school. I still have ruler imprints on my knuckles. I flunked the second grade because I could not learn the alphabet, and I got kicked out of school repeatedly. It was hard on me, and it was hard on my parents.

But I was very lucky to have parents who saw me as an individual. One day, after I was expelled from school at the age of thirteen, the vice principal told my mother not to worry about my future. "Maybe someday he can learn how to lay carpet," he said to console her. I remember my mom came home crying that day and said, "I just know Paul can do more than lay carpets." Mom knew me. She talked to me, and she listened to me. The teachers and administrators only knew what I couldn't do; Mom saw with her own eyes what I *could* do.

See with Your Own Eyes

Seeing for myself is an important theme in my life. I once had a fortune from a fortune cookie that read, "Your eyes believe what they see; your ears believe others." I believe that. Well, reading is just listening with your eyes, right? Good readers collect other people's words; dyslexics tend to see things for themselves. Who is more likely to repeat the ideas of others, and who is more likely to be creative?

Because I couldn't read, I learned from direct experience. Experience is a harsh teacher because the test comes first and the lesson follows. Lacking the ability to learn by reading, I embraced every chance to participate in life. I started businesses, like my vegetable stand. I skipped school to watch my father's stockbroker at work. One thing I saw for myself was that to succeed in school, you had to be good at everything, but to succeed as an adult, you only had to be good at one or two things.

When school had me down, Mom used to tell me that "the A students work for the B students, the C students run the companies, and the D students dedicate the buildings." My experience and observations suggest that she was absolutely right. I'm not recommending that parents say this to a child who's getting As and Bs, but the child who can't play by the same rules needs to know there's much more to life than what goes on a report card. In the workplace, which is more important: your school grades or your ability to forge personal relationships?

Look People in the Eye

To be successful in life is to be engaged with people. We need people. We need to know how to introduce ourselves to them, talk with them, argue with them, and build with them. Yet when I force the college students in my seminar at the University of California Santa Barbara (UCSB) to ask each other out on dates, these young adults do not know how to speak up, express themselves, or look one another in the eye. They may read very well, but they don't know how to talk to each other. They do not want to take chances, but life is full of risk. Since dyslexia prevented me from doing things the conventional way, I grew up experimenting and trying new things. Taking chances became second nature. By forcing students to ask each other out, I give them a crash course in surviving rejection and handling unexpected success.

I learned early that I would only get through school with a lot of help from a lot of people. This dependence taught me how to ask for help and how to provide help when I could. I learned to appreciate people's strengths and forgive their weaknesses, as I hoped they would forgive mine. This was important when I hired my first coworker at Kinko's, but imagine how important people skills were when twenty-five thousand coworkers ran Kinko's?

My longtime coworker Mike Fasth says Kinko's succeeded because nearly every coworker in the company knew the owner. I traveled continuously, visiting stores all over the world. I personally greeted coworkers when they arrived for the company picnic and personally bid them farewell when the event ended. I believe I owe my people skills to dyslexia. Had I been a good reader, with my love of numbers I might well have spent my life as an accountant in a little office somewhere. Instead, I trusted and engaged with other people to imagine and build something larger together.

Use the Mind's Eye

In college, I gathered with friends after a lecture and discovered that although they took detailed notes, I remembered the lecture better. While they were frantically scribbling, I was listening. Coming from the oral tradition, I had developed a good memory.

Plato didn't care much for the rise of literacy in his time, saying, "If men learn this ... they will cease to exercise memory because they rely on that which is written, calling things to remembrance no longer from within themselves, but by means of external marks ... [B]y telling them of many things without teaching them you will make them seem to know much, while for the most part they know nothing, and as men filled, not with wisdom, but with the conceit of wisdom, they will be a burden to their fellows." If you've ever been in a meeting with executives who must consult notes to explain what they are supposedly working on every day, you know that Plato had a very good point.

On the other hand, I know a fellow who, when he cannot remember some detail, says, "My brain is a factory, not a warehouse." Like Sherlock Holmes, this man prides himself on his thinking skills and does not want to treat his brain like a dusty attic full of accumulated bric-a-brac. But good readers have the choice to store information outside their own heads. They can easily look up details they have forgotten. I cannot. Dyslexia forced me to develop my brain into both a factory and a warehouse.

Former Kinko's executive and coauthor Dean Zatkowsky tells this story about my memory. We were dining with some store managers in San Antonio. As I went around the table to greet people, I asked a woman if she had completed her degree and if her husband had fulfilled his dream of starting a game ranch. After I moved on to talk to others, she turned to Dean and excitedly confided that she and I had only spoken once before, three years earlier and for only about five minutes. They were both impressed. He said it demonstrated that I care about people and pay attention to them, two critical traits of leadership. I don't think of this as a strategy, though. It just comes naturally to me, as it would to anyone in a world without writing. It's the kind of memory required for – and developed through – oral communication.

Other business partners used to comment on how well I knew the numbers. Well, I take that for granted; you have to know the numbers. But it took me a long time to realize how hard it was for others to retain details.

I think that filling my brain with so much information stimulates my imagination in a very productive way. The warehouse supplies the factory, so to speak. The facts, figures, and physical observations stored in my brain mix together in creative ways but keep my creativity grounded in reality. In other words, I have a practical imagination. I don't just have dreams – I have ideas.

See Beyond Labels

Remember that scene in *The Matrix* (Groucho II Film Company, 1999) when the little boy bending spoons with his mind tells Neo that he mustn't try to bend the spoon because that's impossible? Instead, the boy explains, you must try to recognize the truth: that there is no spoon. Well, that's how I feel about "the box."

After I became successful, I was praised lavishly for thinking outside the box, even though as a child I was ridiculed, shunned, or even struck for not fitting into the box. Lately, I've heard it said that dyslexics like myself think out of the box because we've never been in the box. I say, "Enough! *There is no box.*"

For people with dyslexia, expressions like learning disability or learning difference – or my own choice, learning opportunity – are simply new boxes to fit people into. How differently would we view the world and ourselves if we saw that the human race consists of 6.6 billion unique individuals? If we did, we'd have to see everyone else more objectively, and we could better appreciate everyone's individual strengths.

In *The Matrix*, the little boy eventually tells Neo that if there is no spoon, it is we who must bend. He means that Neo must open his mind to unlimited possibilities, and I believe we all must do the same. Dyslexia helped me see with my own eyes, learn to look others in the eye, fuel my imagination with everything I saw, and look beyond the labels others applied to me. What I ultimately saw, and believe you can see as well, was a world of endless opportunity.

OWNERSHIP

The Ins and Ons of Ownership

"What does a fish know about the water in which it swims its whole life?" asked Albert Einstein. The question reminds me that we often take for granted the environment essential to our success.

Business owners should ponder two questions: 1) Do you own your business or does it own you? 2) Are you *in* your business or *on* your business?

Several years ago, a very successful freelance writer told us he could never turn down an assignment because if the client found another writer for the task, that writer might get the next assignment. So this writer worked all the time. He never took vacations. Yes, he earned more than most writers, but it seemed to me he had turned his business into a relentless grind, and he lacked the liberty I associate with entrepreneurship. It may have been a necessary phase of business development, but at that point in time, his business owned him.

The distinction between *in* and *on* is the difference between managing tasks and managing the business. You know you are *in* your business when it feels like you are drowning in mundane details every day. My father used to say that the mundane is like a cancer; it eats away at your creativity and prevents you from seeing the bigger picture. As the saying goes, it's hard to think about how to drain the swamp when you're up to your waist in alligators. Being *in* the business means you spend downtime worrying rather than dreaming. Getting *on* your business provides a completely different perspective.

When you step above the frantic daily challenges, you can focus on the three big questions:

1. Are your coworkers motivated?
2. Is your checkbook balanced?
3. Where are your customers going?

To answer these questions, you need time to think. How can you anticipate tomorrow's customer needs when you're obsessed with yesterday's orders? You need motivated coworkers to get the daily work done. Many entrepreneurs face difficulty here, because when you start as a one-person shop, it's very difficult to trust others with the work. But trust allows motivated coworkers to blossom, so if you want to grow, learn to let go.

I don't think you have to do your own bookkeeping to manage cash flow, but I think every business owner can benefit from an accounting class. When it's your money on the line every day, you should be conversant in the language of finance. Because after you learn whether your checkbook is balanced, you'll want to understand why.

When you are *in* your business, you always wish for things to settle down, and you try to fashion policies and systems to help you control the chaos. But when you are *on* your business, you rise above the chaos and see how it can be turned to your advantage. In fact, when you're *on* the business, you constantly stir the pot to keep things mixing and moving. Wherever your customers are going, you want to be there first.

Accountants live in the past, managers live in the present, and leaders live in the future. Get *on* your business, and you'll become the kind of leader who *creates* the future.

Questions:

1. What are you doing to keep your coworkers motivated?
2. How well do you understand your cash flow and tax situation?
3. How can you find out where your customers are going next?

The Toughest Transition for an Entrepreneur

As Kinko's grew, our biggest challenge was moving from a culture of *things* to a culture of *people*. A two-hundred-square-foot store could be operated by one or two people, but there were a lot of machines and systems to master. Copiers, binders, passport photo cameras, film processing procedures, school supplies — these were the things the first store managers had to deal with every day.

Customers were important, of course, but our services were so novel that even the customers were more interested in the *things* that defined Kinko's. Longtime Kinko's coworker and executive Mike Fasth says the early relationship between customers and coworkers was a shared wow! factor. The speed and quality of the equipment blew everybody away. You could get one hundred copies in one minute, and every one of them looked as good — or better — than the original. Eventually, many Kinko's stores were more than five thousand square feet and served over one thousand customers per day, and the store manager was responsible for dozens of coworkers. By then, it was our coworkers, not our machines or processes, that defined Kinko's.

Entrepreneurs often begin by doing everything themselves, but large-scale success requires that they learn how to get things done *through* others. This requires a lot of trust, because if you don't trust others, you still have to do everything yourself.

I think there are some essential steps one must take to move from a culture of things to a culture of people:

I. **Declare your values.** At Kinko's, we promoted the company philosophy and commitments to communication to the extent we were practically begging coworkers to question management's behavior. These documents expressed our expectations of one another, helped coworkers find meaning in their work, and provided a sort of constitution we could turn to when facing difficult decisions. Two of the competencies of leadership, as described by University of Southern California professor Warren Bennis, are managing meaning and managing trust (see *Balance Your Tripod* in the section on Self-Knowledge). A clear declaration of values serves both of these areas. The following two documents appeared as posters in every Kinko's store:

Kinko's Philosophy (circa 1996)

Our primary objective is to take care of the customer. We are proud of our ability to serve him or her in a timely and professional manner, and to provide high quality at a reasonable price. We develop long-term relationships that promote mutual growth and prosperity. We value creativity, productivity, and loyalty, and we encourage independent thinking and teamwork.

Our coworkers are the foundation of our success. We consider ourselves part of the Kinko's family. We trust and care for each other, and treat everyone with respect. We openly communicate our accomplishments and mistakes so we can learn from each other. We strive to live balanced lives in work, love and play. We are confident of our future and point with pride to the way we run our business and treat each other.

Kinko's Commitments to Communication (circa 1996)

1. I will recognize your value to Kinko's.
2. I will share my goals with you, and together we will develop an action plan.
3. I will respect and utilize the chain of command to resolve problems.
4. I will solicit immediate feedback to ensure we understand each other.
5. I will talk with you, not at you.
6. I will listen with an open mind.
7. I will try to see the situation from all points of view.
8. I will tell you when I don't know the answer, and together we will seek the answer.
9. I will give you honest and sincere feedback.
10. I will not usurp your authority.
11. I will not confront you when I am angry.
12. I will not gossip.
13. I will not publicly embarrass you.
14. I will admit when I am wrong.

... and in every case, I am worthy of the same from you.

2. **Manage management.** A culture of people must be a culture of empowered people, so try to maintain a very flat organization chart. Too many levels of management obscure communication, diffuse responsibility, and allow people to avoid thinking for themselves. As has often been said, we should *manage things* and *lead people*. A company with too many managers is treating its people like things.

3. **Celebrate coworkers.** It sounds very cynical when I say, "Give the glory, keep the money," but it's just a funny way of saying, "Give the people what they want." Most people want recognition, and they deserve it. By building both recognition and opportunity into your company's value system, you can share plenty of glory *and money* with the coworkers who desire these things. But no matter what, thank your coworkers loudly and often for their contributions.

Moving from a culture of things to a culture of people is not about feeling warm and fuzzy while singing campfire songs together. It's about building a team that holds similar values and works toward common goals. So it's essential that those values and goals are communicated openly. But an entrepreneur would also do well to remember what Dean's father often said, "It doesn't cost any extra to be nice."

Questions:

1. How do your coworkers know what the company is all about?
2. Do you spend more time working on things or relationships?
3. How do you show appreciation for your coworkers?

The Ultimate Management Skill

Dean prides himself on his hiring skills and says that if you hire people who must be managed, you yourself were a bad hire. He believes that hiring is the ultimate management skill, and I'm inclined to agree.

I've always said that one should manage the environment, not the people. When I talk about managing the environment, I'm usually talking about establishing the values and structure that let ambitious, competent, self-motivated people enthusiastically apply their talents to benefit the organization. But a more basic requirement of managing the environment is to fill it with ambitious, competent, self-motivated people in the first place.

Think about your best, most independent coworker. Now imagine if you had more like him or her. Chapter 9 of *The Essential Drucker* (Harper Business, 2001), a collection of essays by Peter Drucker, is called "Picking People: The Basic Rules," and Dean says he reviews it before every hiring decision.

In addition to making the case for why hiring is the most important management function, Drucker describes the decision-making steps as he sees them, including:

I. **Think through the assignment.** Drucker notes that the job description and the current assignment are not always the same thing. A sales manager who needs to build a new team and one who needs to develop a new territory with an experienced team have different assignments and require different strengths.

2. **Look at a number of potentially qualified people.** Here the emphasis is on the word *number* because out of quantity comes quality. Give yourself real choices. For an executive position, don't be afraid to review two hundred résumés and interview ten to twenty people, some of them repeatedly. This due diligence saves a lot of time in the long run.

3. **Think hard about how to look at the candidates.** Having studied the assignment, focus on the candidates' strengths as they relate to that assignment. Drucker notes that known weaknesses might disqualify a candidate, but "effective executives do not start out by looking at weaknesses. You cannot build performance on weaknesses. You can build only on strengths." What a powerful insight! When Kinko's was rolling its 126 separate partnerships into a single company, many coworkers had to reapply for their existing jobs. Dean took the opportunity to interview many new people for each position. One of his existing coworkers told him quite plainly, "I don't want to be at a disadvantage just because you know my weaknesses. These other candidates have weaknesses too, but our ignorance of them should not be held against me." She was right. Based on

her known strengths (including a forthrightness that he valued highly), she got the job.

4. **Discuss each of the candidates with several people who have worked with him or her.** The experience and opinions of others provide valuable insight about the candidate's *proven* performance and abilities. This reminds me of the old joke about the difference between advertising and public relations (PR). If you tell a woman you're a great lover, that's advertising. If her girlfriends tell her you're a great lover, that's PR, and PR is much more believable than advertising. You'll never meet a racehorse owner who says, "I think my horse is going to lose today," or a company CEO who says, "Well, we're really not very good at what we do." Likewise, you'll rarely interview a candidate who says, "I'm a forgetful, disorganized, micromanaging, mood-swinging tyrant with poor personal hygiene," but if it's true, you'll hear it from his or her coworkers.

5. **Make sure the appointee understands the job.** Here Drucker points out that you must help someone in a new position distinguish between the past performance that got him or her the job and the future performance required to do the job well. *Hiring may be the ultimate management skill, but coworker development is the ultimate management responsibility.*

To these I would add some of my own observations. For one thing, I think credentials often mean very little. Someone can have more degrees than a thermometer, but if he or she is a bad fit for the assignment, failure is a certainty. Don't let an impressive collection of parchments overwhelm your common sense.

When I interview a prospective coworker, I'm trying to get a true picture of the person's attitude, self-discipline, and motivation. And here is where political correctness and I diverge: I always find it useful to have a couple of adult beverages with a candidate, for as the saying goes, in vino veritas—"there is truth in wine." I ask very general questions and let the candidate gab away.

I want to hear how he or she manages money because if someone cannot handle his or her own money responsibly, do I really want that person responsible for mine? I also like to hear about family because you learn a lot about someone's character when you hear about his or her family relationships. After all, you can pick your friends, but you're stuck with your family. How you deal with family says a lot about you. And for long periods of our lives, most of us spend more of our waking hours with coworkers than with family members, so hiring well is not only important for the performance of the organization but also for our personal happiness.

Questions:

1 How many people did you interview for your last opening?
2 How often do you consider your hiring decisions brilliant?
3 Do you have an individual development plan for each new coworker?
4 Are you avoiding dealing with a problem coworker right now? Why?

The Bathroom Test

Can you do business again with a company that won't let you use its bathroom? I recently visited a Border's Bookstore and a Peet's Coffee shop in Marina Del Rey, California, and neither would let me use the bathroom. I was appalled that these otherwise reputable companies treated me so badly.

Bathrooms tell you a lot about a business. A clean bathroom says that the coworkers take pride in their workplace. A well-appointed bathroom tells you that the managers and owners care about their workers. An unavailable bathroom tells you that the business has no respect for you as a human being.

People on the go need to … um … go. The secret to McDonald's early success was the roadside restaurant's hygienic alternative to filthy gas station bathrooms.

A friend tried to excuse Border's and Peet's behavior, noting that he had recently used the public restroom at a very nice hospital, only to find it messy and vandalized. He said companies must get very frustrated when people repay their courtesy with graffiti and broken glass.

Yes, it is frustrating, but meeting and exceeding the expectations of customers is far more important than the relatively minor expense of repairs and cleaning. We intuitively understand that it is wrong to punish everyone for the misdeeds of a few. When a company cannot find a better solution or just bite the bullet and take care of its customers, I'd call it a foolish step toward failure.

Sociologists and municipalities know about the broken-window theory. If you allow broken windows in an impoverished area, the blight increases rapidly. But if you repair broken windows and paint over graffiti quickly, the neighborhood stabilizes and improves. Good leaders take responsibility for these kinds of details. It may seem counterintuitive, but accounting for customer-friendly details is big-picture thinking because these little things reflect the attitude of the organization. Do you think of your customers as human beings or just a long line of wallets waiting to be lightened?

I believe the hospital bathroom was a mess because the administrators do not use that bathroom. Their standards are so high everywhere else in the hospital that it's hard to imagine they would knowingly let visitors have a bad experience at the very front of their building! But they should be aware; it's their responsibility.

At least the hospital made a public restroom available. Retailers who feel I'm good enough to spend money but not good enough to use the bathroom will get a lot less of my money in the future. But they will get a piece of my mind. And a mention in my books, articles, and speeches.

Questions:

1   What amenities do you provide for customers?
2   How often do you inspect the quality of presentation?

3   If you have separate bathrooms for coworkers and customers, how different are they in décor and upkeep? What does each say about your company?

The Secret of Retail Success, or
How To Not Compete

In retail there are few secrets. Ninety percent of what we do and who we are is obvious to customers and competitors alike. Success will be copied, try as you may to prevent it.

Some retailers succeed by copying more innovative competitors, while others succeed through their own continuous innovation. Most employ some combination of idea creation and idea borrowing. It's important to stay aware of one's competition but dangerous to become obsessed. Dean often says that when you focus on the competition, the unintended consequence is parity, but if you focus on customers instead, you are far more likely to innovate and move ahead of the competition.

Creative retailers have the edge, presuming they can market their innovations well enough to capitalize on the product life cycle and benefit from an idea when it is most profitable. The product life cycle simply describes the arc over which a product moves from its beginnings as a profitable novelty, through a mature stage (where it faces increased competition), and to its inevitable decline.

Strategic innovators always have a new product entering the product-profit life cycle just as a previous product begins its competitive decline. By product I also refer to services or, in some cases, novel applications or promotions for mature products. For example, Arm & Hammer Baking Soda® and WD-40® keep discovering and publicizing new uses for their decades-old products to extend the profit life cycle.

Baking soda and WD-40 are important examples because customers and coworkers generously offer most of the new ideas for these two products. Small businesses may feel disadvantaged because they lack marketing departments or high-priced focus group consultants, but they possess something far more valuable—direct access to customers.

Want to read a really great book? It's got everything: drama, conflict, mysteries, and, most of all, uplifting success stories. It's the yellow pages, and it's one of the greatest business textbooks available.

An afternoon leafing through the local phone book provides a master class in positioning, the art of distinguishing—or failing to distinguish—your business from others.

In my opinion, the key to positioning is to never compete. That's right; the best way to beat the competition is by refusing to compete with them. Consider the wisdom of this Grateful Dead bumper sticker: "They're not the best at what they do. They're the only ones who do what they do." Uniqueness should be the objective of every entrepreneur.

When reviewing the yellow pages, you'll see how ad size, images, and language work together to produce an impression of each business. But you must also recognize that a company's very existence suggests they are doing something right. Many small business owners dismiss the competition based on their shortcomings, but this is shortsighted. It's better to give careful consideration to what your competition is doing well.

However, if careful consideration turns to obsession, you're in really big trouble. Companies that obsess over the competition, reacting to every move, aren't competing at all. Rather, they are losing their distinction. Our current political process is a pretty good example: When the candidates focus on each other, they succeed only in dividing the nation. Granted, attacking the competition can be an effective strategy for an inferior company with an insufficient value proposition, but it's an expensive treadmill and such companies eventually succumb to their more innovative competitors.

Innovation springs from listening to customers. In addition to frequent chats with regular customers, you should also interview new customers to learn why they chose you. Even if you already know all the reasons customers might prefer your products or services, it's important to hear it in their own words because *their* language makes the most effective advertising copy.

A hostile newspaper interviewed a Kinko's marketing executive when we were opening a new store in a small community. The paper had already run editorials comparing us to Wal-Mart and claiming we would decimate local businesses. Knowing what he was facing, the Kinko's exec brought phone books from a dozen similar communities where Kinko's already had long-established branches. Each book featured pages and pages of print and copy shops. "There's always a way to succeed," he told the paper, pointing out that Kinko's also started with one small store. "You're either in business for the customers or you're in business for yourself. If you're in business for the customers, you don't have to fear competition." I agree. Businesses do not fail because the competition beat them but because they failed the customer.

If you want your retail business to stay original and successful, make sure you talk to customers every day. Find out what needs and desires are not being met and how much people are willing to pay for them. Use customer language in your signs, ads, and other marketing materials. When your business gets bigger, make sure you also talk to the coworkers who serve customers. And of course, by *talk* I mean ask questions and shut up while they answer.

Entrepreneurs have to fight their natural self-confidence to create a company culture that supports innovation because self-confidence sometimes turns into arrogance. Resist! Resist micromanaging and excessive policy writing! Resist the impulse to ignore criticism. When it's your money on the line, you want to hear all the dirt. After all, which would you rather have, a big ego or a big checkbook?

Questions:

1 How many ways can you get feedback from customers?
2 What makes your company special—not in your mind but in the customer's mind?
3 When you chart the profit life cycle of your products and services, how do you plan for their inevitable decline?

To Increase Productivity, Take More Time Off

Andrei Codrescu's marvelous novel *Wakefield* (Algonquin Books, 2004) features a protagonist who travels the country as a *de-motivational* speaker, hired to depress employees so they will be less creative and just get their work done. It's a hilarious conceit, but if your business depends on healthy, innovative, engaged workers, forget the outside speakers and consider paying coworkers to take longer and more frequent vacations.

Americans average less than half the vacation days taken by citizens of Japan, Korea, Canada, United Kingdom, Brazil, Germany, France, and Italy. According to Joe Robinson's Work to Live Web site (www.worktolive.info), 127 nations have minimum paid-leave laws that protect vacations. Even China, he says, offers three weeks off, apparently as an economic stimulus to get people traveling and spending. Based on their economic growth, the plan appears to be working.

During my years at Kinko's, I worked very long hours, but I also took frequent, long vacations. And when I returned, the first order of business was planning my next vacation. The goal was not to avoid work but to improve my productivity. People do not learn new things and think new thoughts by doing the same things every day for months on end. My vacation schedule also defined firm deadlines for important projects, helping to prioritize my work.

I consider three consecutive weeks a minimum vacation for anyone in a leadership position, and I'll tell you why. If you go away for one week, you come back to an extra week's worth of work. If you're gone for two weeks, you come back to an extra two weeks' worth of work. But if you're gone for three weeks, everyone figures out how to get along without you, and the work gets properly delegated and executed. It's better for you, better for the business, and better for the development of coworkers.

Businesspeople who exercise know they are more likely to have a brainstorm while running than while running a meeting. As the story goes, Isaac Newton was only sitting under the apple tree because his mother told him that instead of helping her on the farm, he should take some time for himself. Unfortunately, many managers understand efficiency far better than they understand effectiveness; they buy people's time rather than invest in their talent.

This efficiency obsession permeates our culture. Americans are such workaholics that we even turn our vacations into type-A stress fests, over-scheduling ourselves and avoiding unstructured time. While visiting the Art Institute of Chicago, a colleague watched visitors flitting through the galleries as if on roller skates. "Cumulatively, I think they looked at their watches and cell phones longer than they looked at any of the art. They had somewhere else to be."

This is a shame because unstructured wandering provides exceptional opportunities for personal growth and education. I think that two days spent meandering through the Art Institute is the educational and inspirational equivalent of a college semester. When you have time to shuffle around the many exhibits, browse the bookstore, people-watch, eavesdrop on the docents, and generally just look around, interesting stuff finds you. For example, Georges Seurat's famous *A Sunday on La Grande Jatte* appeals to art lovers for its colors, shapes, and techniques. But it got me thinking about economics because it depicts a time when leisure was so new to the middle classes that they dressed up in their best clothes just to go to the park. I began to wonder what other artwork might tell me about the economics of the time and place of their creation, leading to new insights for my work in investing.

Real vacations afford adequate time for rejuvenation. Some people advocate legislation to expand and protect paid vacation time, but I think employers will embrace such policies voluntarily when they recognize the bottom-line benefits, such as lower overtime costs, lower absenteeism, lower health-care costs, better cross-training (and therefore better customer service), and higher individual worker productivity. It seems counterintuitive in our work-obsessed society, but longer vacations are good for the employer, the coworker, and the economy.

Questions:

1. How would you rate the quality of your work just before and immediately following your longest vacation?
2. When calculating the cost of vacations to your business, how do you quantify the benefits?
3. Do your coworkers view cross training as professional development or an added burden? If cross training earned coworkers longer vacations, do you think they would enthusiastically learn each other's responsibilities?

Biting the Invisible Hand

A friend recently called me a "capitalist pig." She was joking, but the term is so common it got me thinking about capitalism's PR problem.

A retailer in a university town once told me, "It's hard enough to teach new coworkers about our services, but it's harder when I have to convert them to capitalism first." I view Adam Smith's "invisible hand" as one that beckons with incentives, but some others view it as an iron fist wielding capital like a brutish club. The iron-fist capitalists produce a lot of bad PR, but *embarrassed* capitalists also cause harm. These are the leaders and managers who are ashamed to admit they want to make money.

Embarrassed capitalists operate in an aura of deceit. They try to hide important and perfectly just motives under grandiose mission statements and internal marketing campaigns. In doing so, they disrespect their coworkers' intelligence. Profit is the most important goal of any for-profit organization and should not be marginalized. Rather, profit should be celebrated as the means for achieving every other personal and professional goal sought by the organization, its coworkers, and its customers.

Why do so many people try to obscure the profit motive, as if it were incompatible with the achievement of more personal aspirations?

Some former coworkers raised the question while telling me about their favorite supervisor. Said one, "On my first day, and at every performance appraisal, he gave a speech about making sure the company and I were serving each other's goals. Whether or not your long-term goals included the company, he was very clear: 'You help us reach our goals, and we'll help you reach yours.' But he didn't just talk about it; we built it into the job and held each other accountable. He made my personal goals part of my performance appraisal because he wanted me to be successful!"

That manager understood that good leaders create environments where people's interests are aligned, making day-to-day management downright easy. Most people manage themselves just fine when it's clear where everyone is supposed to be going—and how the journey benefits them.

I have never been shy about my interest in money; I am a money enthusiast. But the best way to make a lot of money is to help people—coworkers and customers—get things they need and want. I learned from experience that kissing coworkers' hands made me more money than slapping them, and that's why I'm such a strong proponent of generous profit sharing.

Iron-fist capitalists see profit distributed to coworkers as money left on the table. They believe that if they *can* take it, it is rightfully theirs. This is shortsighted and counterproductive. Generous profit sharing engages the workforce and wins the owner a slightly smaller piece of a much, much larger pie that has greater cash flow and long-term equity. I've always said that happy fingers ring happy registers. Iron-fist capitalists end up biting the hands that feed them.

And that's why so many workers deride capitalism itself. Their personal experiences suggest the invisible hand is less than benign.

As one humorist put it, "Some see the hand everywhere they look; others see only one finger." Profit sharing makes the invisible hand visible and welcoming, and serves capitalism well.

Questions:

1. How do you communicate your company's financial goals to coworkers?
2. How do you address generational and philosophical differences among your coworkers about the role of business in society?
3. What are the pros and cons of increased profit sharing for your particular organization?

Leadership, Service, and Soul

On a late-night flight across the country, Dean sat between a little old lady who barely spoke English and that little old lady's little old mother, who spoke no English at all. The daughter paid for a two-dollar headset with a ten-dollar bill. The flight attendant said she would return with change. Much later, the lady wished to purchase two five-dollar meals from another attendant and held out a twenty-dollar bill. For a ten-dollar purchase, there was no change for a twenty-dollar bill. The flight attendant seemed paralyzed after the lady explained that another attendant already owed her eight dollars. The headset attendant, who was nearby selling beverages, confirmed this, telling the traveler that if she had two dollars she could have the meals. The increasingly confused lady again held out her twenty-dollar bill. The flight attendants froze.

By this point, Dean had had enough, reached into his pocket, and said, "I'll kick in the two dollars. Just give the ladies their food." The flight attendants hesitated, looking at each other. It was clear they wanted to do the right thing but feared repercussions. He felt they should have just comped the ladies their meals but told me they looked like women who had been reprimanded in the past for helping customers.

For years, the airlines have been running retail businesses during their flights—selling meals and beverages, but without the simple courtesy of ensuring change is available for customers. Apparently, that situation was not inconvenient enough. This airline segments the purchase of headsets, meals, and beverages into distinct categories under the control of specific flight attendants, ensuring that weaknesses in the system affect more people. The recent switch to credit/debit card use on airplanes may help the situation or make it much worse for people who wish to pay with cash, since there will be a smaller pool of customer-provided change.

The ladies got their food, and the headset/beverage attendant gave Dean a couple of free drinks, increasing the irony of the situation. As in too many organizations, it appears that the frontline coworkers were granted little discretion to prevent problems but some power to resolve them. *A generous customer satisfaction policy makes sense, but practice does not make perfect; it just means you get very good at fixing the wrong problems.* This reactive partial empowerment sucks the initiative out of otherwise smart, inventive, and caring coworkers.

I imagine that the airline's CEO does not sit in 38D on the economy flight and thus has little appreciation of the pressures facing his coworkers and customers. Some of his middle managers probably designed a model process for managing in-flight transactions but failed to consider that human beings might be involved in the transactions. In other words, the system was one of those common business practices that only a committee could love—or conceive.

I believe the purpose of management is to remove obstacles; so one purpose of leadership is to prevent, destroy, or circumvent the obstacles created by mediocre or incompetent managers. Remember that management is a job title, but leaders can emerge anywhere in an organization. Leadership isn't about power and bravado; it's a passion for quality that burns in the soul. For the good of the customer, the company, and society, frontline coworkers in any organization have a duty to speak truth to those in power. If company policy inhibits your natural impulse to be kind and generous to two little old ladies who don't speak your language, you need to speak up and change that company policy—or you need to change companies. Otherwise, the damage a job like that does to your psyche will hamper the rest of your career and rob the rest of us of your best efforts.

Questions:

1. However great your product or service, what little stumbling blocks might be impacting your customer service? In Jan Carlzon's book about how he rebuilt Scandinavian Airlines, he called these points of customer interaction "moments of truth." (Moments of Truth, Collins Business, 1989)
2. How often do you put yourself into your customers' shoes?
3. How much authority do coworkers have to immediately resolve customer service issues?

JUDGMENT

You, the Jury

It's a shame so many people—especially entrepreneurs—avoid jury duty. For one thing, if people like you avoid jury duty, who will be on the jury if *you* get into trouble? For another, jury duty provides a powerful refresher course in the process of judgment. This is really important because the workplace tests our judgment every day.

Dean recently spent a day in the jury selection process for a criminal trial. Certainly the exercise was tedious but also fascinating. The attorneys repeated the same questions over and over again, focusing on a prerequisite skill for anyone in a position of authority: Can you distinguish fact from opinion?

Each prospective juror was asked to describe how he or she resolved conflicts between children or coworkers who presented disparate accounts of events. I think we all cringe at the prospect of having to judge a he said /she said type of conflict, but such events are common in the workplace. If all the facts were indisputable and available for consideration, we could use a computer rather than a jury to render a judgment. Judges admonish jurors to consider only the facts, but the issue has gone to trial because the facts are in dispute. Still, the discipline reinforced on jury duty is to *start with the facts, such as they are.*

Of course, facts are always skewed by perception. In photography, there is a situation known as parallax, when, for example, the camera's viewfinder sits an inch or so above the lens. That means the photographer and the camera see the subject from slightly different angles; so the resulting photograph will not be *true* to what the photographer saw. As one moves closer or farther from the subject, the disparity increases or decreases.

Likewise, two witnesses will see an event differently based on their own literal and figurative points of view, and someone who hears their testimony adds his or her own point of view to the mix. That's why we need so many people on juries—to compare points of view and come to a consensus about the facts. And that's why business decision makers need committees, advisory boards, or spousal sounding boards to test their thinking. It's vital to see things with your own eyes when possible, but it is also important to try to see them through others' eyes.

Good judgment requires the encouragement of our skepticism and the discouragement of our cynicism. A skeptic questions opinions and looks for factual verification, whereas a cynic assumes self-serving motives behind every action. The cynic forms opinions in advance of the facts.

A responsible juror must form an opinion about the facts but must avoid theorizing in advance of the facts. Dean used to have a bumper sticker that said, *Don't believe everything you think*. That's a useful philosophy because entrepreneurs make decisions every day, and the quality of those decisions will depend to some extent on their ability to question their own opinions. The challenge is to become your own best skeptic without destroying your ability to decide.

Thus, another valuable lesson from jury duty comes with the judge's discussion of *reasonable doubt*. In criminal cases, prospective jurors are frequently reminded of the difference between a reasonable doubt and any doubt. Anyone who has served on a jury knows that some people never get it. But for an entrepreneur, this distinction can prevent analysis paralysis. We cannot eliminate all doubts before we act, so we need a standard for evaluating the reasonableness of our concerns.

Jury duty exercises our ability to distinguish fact from opinion and makes us consider how we set the bar for overcoming doubt. We also benefit by reflecting on the concept of duty. Many of the people who tried to get out of Dean's jury pool claimed hardship but presented mere inconveniences as their excuse. The judge's exasperation seemed to have no effect on them. Dean found this a bit depressing because he views the justice system as one of our greatest achievements and greatest necessities. An understanding of duty is an understanding of priorities, and priorities determine what gets done and what does not. Moreover, duty is a source of honor.

An entrepreneur takes on a duty to serve customers and coworkers. This sense of duty guides his or her judgment in day-to-day decision making. So does the discipline to always start with the facts and the ability to disregard unreasonable doubts. A businessperson on jury duty recognizes that we cannot get all the facts and our judgment will always be imperfect, but often we must decide anyway. That's how leaders keep a business moving forward.

A thoughtful participant can get a lot out of jury duty. So the next time you receive a summons, don't look at it as a burden but rather as a free self-improvement workshop.

Questions:

1. How do you resolve conflicts when friends or coworkers present conflicting accounts of events?
2. When analyzing the pros and cons of a new idea, what is your standard for reasonable doubt? Do you assign probabilities to potential outcomes?
3. What are your duties as a businessperson? As a family member? As a citizen?

The Leader Paints While the Manager Takes Snapshots

During the last quarter of the nineteenth century, many impressionist painters developed a strong hostility toward the art of photography. In the 1870s, Eadweard Muybridge developed fast camera shutters, more sensitive film emulsions, and remote-control devices to trip his new shutters. As a result, he was able to freeze the motion of people and animals, and capture the motion of a fraction of a second, faster than the blink of an eye.

Muybridge's first images, which settled a bet about whether all four of a trotting horse's legs were ever off the ground at the same time, caused many painters to reassess their depictions of animals in motion. Muybridge revealed details previously invisible to the naked eye.

But this was exactly why the impressionist painters labeled photography *unrealistic*, fraudulent, a lie. They made the point that photography may be able to stop time, but time itself never stops, and therefore an impressionistic painting provides a truer image of life than a photograph. The impressionists wished to capture—and communicate—the whole experience of a scene.

Entrepreneurs know that the impressionist painters were onto something. Time does not stop, so every hour of every day introduces new ambiguities into the running of a business. *Innovation becomes a reflex in organizations that embrace this ambiguity.* Some managers try to eliminate ambiguity through research reports, spreadsheets, and other snapshots, keeping themselves so busy looking backward that they don't have time to think about what's ahead.

Your business is in constant motion and constantly connected to— and interdependent with—a million constantly changing factors. Understanding the motion and sensing the consequences of those connections requires an impressionist's vision.

Continuous change does not require a frantic, espresso-fueled management style. On the contrary, I think a leader achieves calm by accepting the reality of continuous change. In company cultures that embrace the inevitability of change, innovation becomes habitual rather than crisis-driven; the business adapts organically to its changing environment. People who are uncomfortable with ambiguity always search for a unified field theory of work that is some combination of policies and systems that will settle the daily routine once and for all. Routine is fine in a world that doesn't change.

After he left Kinko's, Dean became the marketing vice president for a public company. Two of his coworkers spent each morning compiling intricate reports about the previous day's advertising. Dean could not understand the purpose of these reports, so he met with each of the five executives who received them. None of the executives read the reports; each assumed someone else needed them. At some point in the company's history, the daily advertising reports may have been necessary, but they had long since become a mere ritual with no meaning or purpose. Two hardworking, competent coworkers were devoting half of each day to frantically organizing data, but it took an outsider to question how these snapshots served—or failed to serve—the business.

Too many businesspeople are "data-holics," believing they can see an entire company in a snapshot report. Spreadsheets and reports are most useful when recognized for what they are—a collection of data representing a mere sliver of time. The data is useful within its limits, but data is not information, information is not knowledge, and knowledge is not wisdom. Understanding requires our thoughtful, creative, and intuitive interpretation.

The toughest thing in business is managing ambiguity, but it's also the reality of business. To face that reality, see like an impressionist painter—not a documentary photographer.

Questions:

1. How useful is the time you devote to creating or reviewing reports?
2. What other daily activities are rituals of questionable utility?
3. How can you help coworkers become more adaptable to daily ambiguity?
4. What factors represent the grass, trees, and boulders in the painting of your business? In other words, what changes at the slightest breeze, what could be felled by a strong gust, and what withstands all but the most cataclysmic events? How does seeing this help you organize and prioritize your daily work?

Unresolved Issues

Long ago, in a Zen monastery, a distraught monk approached his priest. "Oh, wise master," said the monk, "I am a failure. I have meditated and meditated but cannot achieve enlightenment." His master smiled reassuringly and said, "This will pass." One year later, the same monk bounded joyfully into his master's chambers. He said, "Oh, wise master, I have done it! I have achieved enlightenment!" His master smiled reassuringly and said, "This will pass."

The master's philosophy certainly applies to business. Today's headache often leads to tomorrow's brainstorm, and whenever we think we've finally nailed it, and business can go nowhere but up, new challenges appear. The Zen master, like the vigilant entrepreneur, accepts the inevitability—and unpredictability—of change. Owning a business requires that we learn how to go to sleep with unresolved issues.

An associate of mine steadfastly refused to start his own business for many years, claiming he didn't have the stomach for it. He was wise to recognize the central role of one's stomach in business. He finally became an entrepreneur when he realized that he didn't necessarily need a *strong* stomach, but one that rumbles loudly.

As I explain to students, if your brain falls in love with someone but your heart does not, you get a stomachache. If your heart falls in love but your brain does not, you get a stomachache. Your stomach is the center of wisdom, subconsciously balancing the arrogance of your head and heart, so listen to your stomach!

Trusting your stomach is not a matter of shooting from the hip and acting on intuition; rather, it is the policy of drawing on your experience and inviting intuition to the conference table. If you've done the math and a deal still *feels* wrong, you owe it to yourself to find out why.

Experience doesn't just improve your skills—it educates your gut and refines your radar. However, a rumbling stomach is no excuse for paralysis. An entrepreneur must learn to act in spite of ambiguity. You'll make good decisions, and you'll make bad decisions. You'll make good decisions that go bad. But, as Winston Churchill said, "if you're going through hell, keep going." *I'm not saying that any action is better than no action, but I am saying that inaction should be a conscious choice and not a result of indecision or analysis paralysis.*

Accepting the inevitability of change frees your stomach to worry about other things. To succeed in business, we must learn how to go to sleep with unresolved issues, because as Gilda Radner's Roseanne Rosanadana used to say, "It's always something."

Going to bed with unresolved issues also presents an opportunity to tap the creative powers of our subconscious minds. Consider how two of America's greatest writers exploited (and overcame) anxiety to improve their work. Ernest Hemingway explained that part of his process was to quit writing *before* he was finished each day. That is to say, he stopped writing in the middle of a paragraph when he still had plenty to write. In doing so, he knew exactly how to get started the next morning, and we all know how difficult it can be to get started. Since Hemingway knew what he'd be doing first thing in the morning, his mind was free to explore elsewhere.

Ray Bradbury is not only one of our best writers but also one of our most prolific. Yet, he writes only two hours a day, always first thing in the morning. He spends the rest of each day "filling the well," experiencing life so he has things to write about. Knowing his subconscious mind will continue working while he sleeps, Bradbury gives it assignments at bedtime. He goes over any problems he's having with characters, plots, or language; insists that his subconscious take care of it by morning; and then drifts happily off to sleep. In the morning, he awakens with fresh ideas and gets to work.

Stress comes with owning a business. Learning to sleep with unresolved issues ensures that you'll face each day's new challenges with an alert and creative mind.

Questions:

1. Are you more adept at avoiding stress, ignoring stress, capitulating to stress, or using stress to enhance your creativity?
2. Can you think of an instance when not listening to your stomach got you in trouble?
3. How often have events that seemed like crises when you were tired turned out to be nothing once you were rested?

The Midas Touch

On a television documentary several years ago, an audiologist presented findings of significant hearing damage to a fan of loud music. The music enthusiast reviewed the researcher's findings and came to his own conclusion: He would have to install more powerful amplifiers in his car. The researcher—and everyone who watched the program, I'm sure—stared slack jawed as the music lover thanked the audiologist for discovering that he would need higher volume to compensate for the hearing damage loud music had caused. Obviously, people hear what they want to hear, even if they cannot hear very well.

I've noticed that we often misinterpret cautionary tales. We say someone has "the Midas touch" when he or she experiences frequent success, even though the story of King Midas is the story of a curse. Midas was already wealthy and successful when he greedily sought more. His "golden touch" destroyed everything he loved. To me, the story of King Midas is more than a warning against greed; it's a reminder that fortunes are lost in the good times, when self-confidence crosses the line into hubris. (Remember hubris? It's the excessive pride that always led to tragedy in Greek mythology and drama.)

For organizations and individuals, good judgment and frugality can be the first casualties of success. We've all heard about prizefighters and lottery winners who go bankrupt shortly after winning millions. Many of us have experienced the strange phenomenon that no matter how quickly our income increases, our spending increases just as fast. A little bit of success gets people thinking everything they touch will turn to gold. So individuals start buying fancy cars and summer homes, and companies start buying fancy buildings and other companies.

On the one hand, it's perfectly appropriate for successful entrepreneurs to throw some loose nickels around and invest in prospective opportunities. On the other hand, one must maintain a habit of frugality with both money and self-congratulatory pride. We want our businesses to grow, but, as environmentalist writer Edward Abbey said, "growth for the sake of growth is the ideology of the cancer cell." More important to the success of our businesses is that *we* continue to grow as leaders by admitting our mistakes and learning from them.

Peter Lynch (*One Up on Wall Street*, Simon & Schuster, 1989) coined the term *diworsification* to describe a company's self-destructive tendency to expand into realms beyond its competency. How many troubled companies have started a turnaround by declaring that "from now on, we're going to stick to the knitting"? Except for excessive pride, they might have stuck to their core competency in the first place.

Sticking to the knitting is not about avoiding experiments. It's about knowing your business cold, especially the economic drivers that can be further developed. Before adding new products or services, you must determine whether they are complementary and synergistic, or distracting and draining.

After turning all his food and even his beloved daughter to gold, King Midas begged the gods to save him from his "gift." They did, and although he no longer had the Midas touch, he regained his quite satisfactory life as a just king and loving father, but with a little bit more wisdom as well.

In *Good to Great*, Jim Collins describes the Level 5 Leaders who helped good companies turn into great organizations that outperformed all their peers over time. One characteristic of these Level 5 Leaders was humility. They were ambitious people with great egos, but their egos were tied to the performance of the company – not self-aggrandizement. Fortunes are lost in the good times because we become too full of ourselves. We still tell the stories of King Midas, Icarus (who flew too close to the sun), and Jeff Skilling (who thought everything Enron touched would turn to gold) for the same reason we remember the Bible verse "Pride cometh before destruction, and a haughty spirit before a fall." We're supposed to learn from the collective experience of our forebears.

Questions:

1. How recently has overconfidence gotten you in trouble?
2. In your own business, how have you diversified? Diworsified?
3. What is the central profit generator for your business? How do you keep it top of mind while considering new products, services, or processes?

Clever Is Fine, but Clear Is Final

While I agree with Mark Twain's famous comment that the difference between the right word and the almost-right word is the difference between lightning and the lightning bug, I would add that the right word is the simplest word that gets the job done. Consider this the next time you prepare a business presentation.

A lot of people equate eloquence and intelligence, so they turn to the thesaurus and bring out the big guns when they want to sound smart. Unfortunately, this is also the technique of the con man. All else being equal, if you cannot present your idea in clear, simple language, I smell a rat.

I'm not suggesting you must dumb down presentations. However, I believe that the best way to show respect for the audience's intelligence is to show respect for their time. I go to so many meetings at which the presenter *assumes* no one has prepared and then proceeds to "present" by reading slides verbatim. Worse, he or she sticks to the carefully prepared program for fifty minutes of an hour meeting, eliminating the possibility of meaningful dialogue. If you really have something of value to sell, let the audience sell it to themselves through their questions.

Of course, when you lack an offer of real value, there's always PowerPoint. When I have the authority to do so, I forbid PowerPoint presentations because the program invites excess. Certainly there is an art to persuasive presentation, but sacrificing clarity for artifice degrades communication. Listeners need to rebel against fancy presentations and demand clear, concise executive summaries.

For some reason, every advertising agency presentation I've sat through seemed to include the entire history of advertising, a multimedia extravaganza, a step-by-step explanation of why advertising *seems* immeasurable to the ignorant and uninitiated—and all of this explained with the highest jargon-to-English ratio possible. As Sam Spade said in *The Maltese Falcon*, "the cheaper the hood, the gaudier the patter." Or, as I like to put it, the less one has to offer, the fancier the presentation.

I've got nothing against cleverness, but when I'm evaluating a business decision or an investment opportunity, my BS detector is very sensitive, and flowery language sets off alarms. I need information, clearly stated in plain English. Most business owners and investors tell me they want the same thing. I think that's why we are finally seeing a PowerPoint backlash. PowerPoint is a good tool that has been mercilessly abused by multitudes of mediocre middle managers who value style over content.

When I agree to listen to a presentation, I want to be convinced, not bedazzled. If they can't say it in plain English, I don't work with them.

Questions:

1. What's the most effective presentation you've seen? Why?
2. What's the most effective presentation you've given? Why?

3. What steps do you take to prevent yourself from buying or investing in something you do not fully understand?

You Can't Make Money While You're Running Scared

"Don't look back; something might be gaining on ya!" —Satchel Paige

I come from a long line of entrepreneurs. Growing up, I never knew anyone who had a job; everyone I knew owned his own business. When my mother said, "You can't make money while you're running scared," she was sharing the wisdom of careful observation. She had watched generations of entrepreneurs and understood the difference between those with the courage to grow and change, and those who desperately tried to defend what they already had.

At Kinko's, I saw examples of both styles. Some partners aggressively expanded, taking chances to open more stores, serve more customers, and make more money. On rare occasions, these partners overextended themselves, but in the long run, they prospered. Others started making some money with one or two stores and focused their efforts on protecting that revenue stream. They didn't expand because they felt it was too expensive. But it wasn't too expensive for the competition. Instead of protecting what they had, my partners' defensive postures often caused their businesses to shrink.

There's a fine line between courage and recklessness, and to their credit, many entrepreneurs cannot distinguish this line. Often, the difference is just a matter of twenty-twenty hindsight anyway. If you bet right, the move was courageous. If you bet wrong, you were reckless. Fortunately, entrepreneurs often turn a deaf ear to other people's negativity. We have been told, "It can't be done," "There's no market for a home computer," and "You cannot sell Xerox copies for pennies."

It takes a lot of courage to start your own business, a lot of courage to stick with the business in tough times, and even more courage to change the business before it is necessary.

An entrepreneur must err on the side of trying new things. At Kinko's, our mistakes cost almost nothing because the core business was profitable enough to sponsor experiments. So we had one thousand laboratories trying new services, new products, and new methods of production. Knowing the core business could not sustain us forever, we reinvested those profits to help us discover the next source of profits.

Yet another kind of courage is required after you try things: the courage to recognize failure and move on. William Faulkner was a fearless, sometimes wildly experimental author. He advised writers of the need to "kill your darlings." For example, sometimes you open an essay with a really witty sentence, but as the essay develops, the sentence no longer fits. It can be very hard for writers to cut that sentence, but it must be sacrificed for the quality of the whole.

Business owners know the feeling. You launch a new product that you really believe in. You give it lots of support and every chance to succeed, but it doesn't take off. Instead, it starts to degrade the morale of coworkers and your attention to other business needs.

Do you have the courage to pull the plug, or do you let it linger too long and drag down everything around it?

Recklessness is a true danger, so one must build a margin of safety into each new venture. The margin of safety answers the question *what's the worst that could happen?* If the worst is unbearable, don't go there. But if the potential losses are tolerable and the potential gains are exciting, why not give it a shot?

You cannot make money while you're running scared; you have to take some bold chances to grow your business. And sometimes you have to boldly abort a failed experiment. Don't let the failures dampen your enthusiasm for experimentation, because it's the owner's job to look forward, not back.

Questions:

1. How many new products or services did you try last year?
2. How many products or services did you eliminate last year?
3. How do you encourage new ideas from coworkers and customers?

SELF-KNOWLEDGE

Balance Your Tripod

I gave a lot of speeches during my thirty years at Kinko's, and nearly every one of them included a reference to the tripod of work, love, and play. I would rest three fingers on the podium to illustrate the strength and stability when all three legs of a tripod were of equal length. I didn't tell coworkers how to find balance in their lives, but I constantly reminded them that balance was important, and that the company *knew* it was important.

Most people think they can impress the boss simply by working harder, like the horse in George Orwell's *Animal Farm*. But nothing impresses the boss like results, and the best results come from people with balance and perspective. Personally, I would rather *think* hard than work hard.

At Kinko's, the value of a balanced life was reinforced through our training and educational programs. An article by USC professor Warren Bennis was an important document in defining the Kinko's culture. It was about the "Four Competencies of Leadership." We held workshops on the four competencies at Kinko's University, and I still believe they provide a great touchstone for people who wish to be good leaders, regardless of title, scope of authority, or personal style.

The four competencies are:

1) managing attention,
2) managing meaning,
3) managing trust, and
4) managing yourself.

In a nutshell, *managing attention* means that you cannot lead people who aren't listening, so you need strategies for getting their attention. Some leaders use outrageous antics; I've heard that Mo Siegel of Celestial Seasonings entered a company meeting on the back of an elephant. That would have gotten my attention. Others use the quiet authority of visible day-to-day competency in the workplace—David Packard spent much of each day roaming the lab and factory floors of Hewlett-Packard. Whatever your style, you have to call people's attention to your vision.

Managing meaning requires communication skills that help followers understand the purpose of the organization and their roles in it. Leaders achieve this by viewing communication as a covenant rather than a contract. In a contract, each party might take a 50 percent share of responsibility. So, if communication were a contract, I might speak and consider my work done, since it's your job to hear and understand. But if communication is a covenant, each party carries 100 percent responsibility, so the leader not only speaks but must also ensure understanding.

I define *managing trust* as doing what you say you're going to do, pure and simple. Of course, it's not as easy as it sounds, but without trust, there is no followership, and without followership, there is no leadership.

My tripod speeches were about *managing yourself.* Too many aspiring executives work themselves haggard and anxious, but most of us do not aspire to be haggard and anxious, so why would we want to follow such people? It's okay to take a lunch break. It's okay to go pick up your dry cleaning. It's okay to go on a date and turn off your cell phone. A good business shouldn't kill you.

Some people emphasize love or play too much, but usually it is work that comes to dominate an individual in our culture. Please remember that an unbalanced tripod is inherently unstable, and when it tips too far, the entire tripod falls.

I'm very proud of the fact that many married couples worked together at Kinko's, and our divorce rate was much, much lower than the national average. Sadly, some of these couples divorced after they left Kinko's. I wonder if our constant reminders to balance work, love, and play as if each had a minimum daily requirement helped these people appreciate each other. I believe it takes a village to accomplish great things, and we need to recognize the workplace as one type of modern village. If so, the owner/mayor/chief bears responsibility for the well-being of his or her people and must lead by example.

Questions:

1. Have talented coworkers in your organization regularly resisted promotions to positions of greater responsibility?
2. How would you rate yourself on the four competencies of leadership? How would you rate your most effective coworker on the same traits?

3. You may have heard this one before, but what does it avail a man to gain the world and lose his soul?

4. What can you do today to better balance your tripod of work, love, and play?

What Are You Listening For?

Winston Churchill said, "Courage is what it takes to stand up and speak. Courage is also what it takes to sit down and listen."

True, but courage alone does not make a good listener.

Many people listen wrong because they lack respect for others. Now, some insist that respect must first be earned, but I disagree. If we start by showing respect for everyone, those who don't deserve it will quickly find ways to lose the honor, but we'll have many more opportunities to appreciate and learn from others along the way.

When we respect another, we listen for the truth and meaning in what the other person says, even if we have to use a large strainer to filter out less desirable material. But an awful lot of people have been trained to listen first for error and offense, and to stop listening when either appears. This is unfortunate because errors are common and offense could be unintended. *Our society has chosen to forget that unintended offense should not be offensive at all.* As Christopher Hitchens reminds us in his *Letters to a Young Contrarian* (Basic Books, 2005), one definition of a gentleman is someone who is never rude except on purpose.

Of this you can be sure: If you listen for error and offense, you will surely find them. Of this you can also be sure: If you listen for truth and meaning, you will surely find them.

When someone cheerfully says, "Happy holidays!" or "Merry Christmas!" do you honestly believe he or she intends to offend you? Why then, do so many people choose to be offended? Because many people, especially those with broadcast soapboxes, love to be offended. You know the type: They get up every morning wondering what they can be angry about today. They've created a "semantic-phobia" in our culture, a cynical style of listening as if every word from everyone else is merely an attempt to harm or trick us.

I'd like to share with you a bit of wisdom from my youth that might help you: Sticks and stones can break my bones, but words will never hurt me. Now, we all know that words *can* hurt—the popular psychology "experts" won't let us forget that fact. But here's my belief: Words can only hurt you if you let them.

By the way, not everyone out there is trying to trick you. Listening for truth and meaning filters out the rare tricksters just as effectively as listening for error and offense, but it also allows one to learn new things along the way.

* * *

From *Pee-wee's Big Adventure* (Warner Bros., 1985):

Simone: I know you're right, Pee-wee, but . . .
Pee-wee: Everyone I know has a big "but" . . . C'mon, Simone, let's talk about your big "but" . . .

How can you tell when someone is *not* listening for truth and meaning? One sign is the expression *yeah, but*, which suggests that one has listened only for something to contradict. My coauthor, Dean, calls the expression *yeah, but* a reflexive rebuttal, a knee-jerk need to trump another's point with one of your own.

We should revise the expression *no ifs, ands, or buts*. There's nothing wrong with *ifs* and *ands*. *Ifs* are dreams. *Ands* are inclusive. But, *buts*? Get your but out of here. *But* is too often a weasel word, an introduction to an excuse or a plea for escape. People say *but* on the way to saying no. Like Pee-wee suggested, we weigh down our ideas with our big buts.

Before you reflexively counter someone's statement, or your own, find something within it to affirm. See if you can get through your next business debate, dinner conversation, or daydream without falling back on your big *but*.

* * *

Churchill understood well that a good leader must face bad news squarely and listen attentively to things he or she does not want to hear. He also understood that comfort with paradox and ambiguity is evidence of a mind trained for learning and growth. Well before World War II, Churchill lavished praise on Hitler and Mussolini for the progress and pride they had brought to their desperate nations. During the war, he cursed them emphatically. He could acknowledge the good they had done without blinding himself to how badly it had all gone.

To accomplish more in our businesses, we need the ability to debate important issues without disregarding the other person's point of view. Remember Lyndon Johnson's observation that "if two men agree on everything, you can be sure that one of them is doing the thinking"? We need open, honest dissent to make sure we're encouraging new ideas.

But to benefit from conflict and dissent, we must listen. Listening for error and offense merely confirms what we already believe and renders us unable to understand what the other wishes to communicate; we learn nothing listening that way. The search for truth and meaning leads to new insights, ideas, and inspiration. What are you listening for?

Questions:

1. Do you really listen to your coworkers, or do you use their speaking time to prepare your response?
2. What's the best idea you've gotten from someone else?
3. What's the best idea you got from someone else but initially dismissed?

A Hidden Lesson from the Subprime Fiasco

An article in the February 7, 2008, issue of the *New York Times* included this sentence, "When faced with losses, individuals may seek to take more risk rather than less, contrary to what traditional economic thought might suggest."

That sentence bothered me. I understand risk aversion; people fear losses more than they appreciate gains, and this causes ordinary people to do the wrong thing at the wrong time. They sell when prices are down and buy when prices are up. Risk aversion degrades people's judgment in financial matters; that's a fact. But that's not what bothered me about the sentence in the *Times*. The part of the sentence that got me was the reference to "traditional economic thought."

How many people behave contrary to traditional economic thought simply because they are not conversant in traditional economic thought? Talk to one hundred teenagers, and I doubt you will meet more than one who has received any formal instruction on how to manage money. Talk to one hundred middle-aged Americans, and the number improves; you might find five people who have taken a finance class or investing seminar. Everyone else seems to learn by word of mouth, and trial and error. Mostly error.

Even though our adult lives are dominated by financial decisions, we have neither required nor equipped our schools to properly instruct *all* children about cash flow, debt, interest rates, taxes, investments, buying a house, etc.

America's subprime mortgage fiasco grew as large as it did because millions of borrowers had no idea what they were doing, and bankers drunk with greed were eager to exploit the situation. Many ill-informed homebuyers and refinancers will be paying a steep price for their ignorance, but so will our society. For this reason, it is essential that we bring comprehensive financial literacy instruction into our school systems.

On March 4, 2008, the New *York Times* ran a great article called "Unlike Consumers, Companies Are Piling Up Cash." Apparently, corporate balance sheets were the brightest spot in the economy at that time. Some companies had enough cash on hand to pay off all of their debt. They didn't have to because they bought the debt cheap. Cheap debt and large cash reserves gave the companies tremendous flexibility.

Cash makes a company more agile, better able to adapt to changing conditions. But look at the headline again—specifically the words "Unlike Consumers." With our negative savings rate, the American people have decided to emulate our government instead of our better businesses; we borrow against presumed future income rather than save and invest money to build wealth. If I could get one idea across to people young and old, it would be this: *Save some money!* (Note: The best-case scenario over time is to build a bulletproof portfolio that provides interest, dividends, rent, and liquidity.)

I don't recommend stuffing cash into a mattress; I'm a big believer in putting one's money to work, with a goal of personal solvency.

Personal solvency creates choices—the ability to start a business, get your existing business through tough times, or to leave a job you hate to try something new.

Benjamin Franklin said that when you borrow money, you give power over your life to someone else. American companies that accumulated cash were able to preserve their freedom. How about you?

A friend of mine says that Republicans accept that some people will fall through the cracks, Democrats believe we must help everyone who falls through the cracks, and entrepreneurs believe we should fix the cracks. So here's my entrepreneurial suggestion for reducing the severity of our periodic economic crises: require financial literacy courses in elementary school, middle school, high school, and college. Love of money may be the root of all evil, but ignorance of money is not much better.

* * *

"I talk to myself but I don't listen ..." —Elvis Costello

Of course, education isn't everything. Let's assume for a moment that every purchase is an investment. That assumption is one of the key differences between people who understand money and people who do not because every purchase *is* an investment. Whether you are choosing a car, a camera, a licorice rope, or a company's stock for your IRA, you should *always* try to get maximum value for your money. Getting good value requires *information and discipline*.

Gathering information is easy. We are blessed today with easy access to lots of information. Satellite television and time-shifting DVRs give us access to news and commentary from all over the world.

We can find podcasts and Internet forums covering any type of investment or purchase we are considering.

Have you looked at iTunes University? It's fantastic. Anyone with a computer and Internet connection now has access to a wide variety of college courses from reputable campuses, free of charge.

There are also organizations like the Teaching Company, which sells complete audio and video courses. For less than the cost of an annual parking permit at most college campuses, you can *own* a complete course on the history of philosophy or any other subject that fires your imagination. Lifelong learning is easier than ever.

With so much information and accumulated knowledge at our fingertips, it should be much easier to make quality decisions, shouldn't it? But what good is all this information if we lack the self-discipline to control our impulses? I know a fellow who consults *Consumer Reports* before every purchase, carefully decides which item is best for his needs and his budget, and then, when he's ready to buy and the item is out of stock, he impulsively buys whatever similar item he can get immediately. He talks to himself, but he doesn't listen.

The greatest entrepreneurial discipline is the willingness to face the facts, admit the facts, and act on the facts. And make no mistake: Managing your personal finances is an entrepreneurial endeavor.

So when the marketing-driven impulse for recreational shopping strikes, can we stop long enough to ask: 1) Do I really need it? 2) Can I afford it? If either answer is no, we should hesitate and try to find an alternative. For the last thirty years, people have been answering both questions with no and making the purchase anyway.

We talk to ourselves, but we don't listen. In the long run, we have only debt to show for our hard work.

I'm a big fan of intuition and spontaneity, but I'm also a big fan of thoughtful deliberation. When it comes to asking someone out on a date, go ahead and be spontaneous. But when it comes to spending money, be thoughtful and deliberative. Bankers did not create our economic crisis alone; they were abetted by people who were eager to buy junk they didn't need with money they didn't have. We have been part of the problem; can we find the discipline to be part of the solution?

Questions:

1. How and when did you learn about money?
2. What was your first big financial mistake?
3. What was your worst financial mistake?
4. Was the mistake caused by an error of knowledge or a failure of discipline? Or both?

Real Performance Requires Real Fuel

Dean sometimes offers this explanation of society's woes: "We are what we eat, but we don't know what we're eating, so we don't know who we are."

I cannot vouch for the entire sentiment, but he's absolutely right that we don't know what we're eating. Nancy Deville wrote a fascinating book called *Death by Supermarket* (Barricade Books, 2007). She describes in considerable detail how certain chemical compounds—notably high fructose corn syrup (HFCS) and monosodium glutamate (MSG)—have infiltrated nearly every so-called "food" available in the inner aisles of our supermarkets. (Thoughtful shoppers know that real foods—produce, meat, and dairy—are on the perimeter of the store.)

Most of us have no idea how much HFCS and MSG we consume, but we know we are hungry, right now, for something that tastes really good. Americans eat so much that we have an obesity epidemic; why then are we always hungry? Much of America's weight problem can be traced to the addictive qualities of HFCS and MSG. These chemical compounds unnaturally boost your blood sugar, which then drops quickly, leaving you moody, fuzzy minded, and hungry. We've made calories very cheap and very addictive; factory foods are the crack cocaine in every pantry.

Some readers of Nancy's book see evidence of conspiracy. I believe that what we often mistake for conspiracy is just the cumulative effect of individual acts of greed. Factory food is more profitable than real food, so market forces encourage its production. Legendary investor and presidential adviser Bernard Baruch once pointed out that wars are started for a wide variety of reasons, but they last as long as they do because they're so darn profitable. The war profiteers do not advocate war per se, but when the cash is rolling in, they support the status quo. I believe it's the same with factory foods: There's no conspiracy, just entrepreneurialism without scruples. The net result is the same: Poisons disguised as food keep rolling off the assembly line. Perhaps this is a necessary evil of liberty, but as individuals, we also have the liberty to rebel.

Government intervention in the fake-food business is no more likely than government interference in the military-industrial complex, so individuals must wage the campaign for real food as a guerrilla offensive. Education is weapon number one.

Education of the public is off to a good start. Best-selling books like Michael Pollan's *The Omnivore's Dilemma* (Penguin, 2007) and Barbara Kingsolver's *Animal, Vegetable, Miracle* (Harper Perennial, 2008) remind people that real food is healthier than processed foods and no less convenient once they straighten out their priorities. When we break our dependency on highly addictive substances like HFCS and MSG, we can again relish the flavors of natural foods, a pleasure that has motivated mankind from the beginning of time.

When I was a kid, school filmstrips showed astronauts of the future living on vitamin pills and protein paste from a tube. It actually looked pretty cool, certainly no worse than broccoli at home. But now we know that our bodies are not designed for manufactured food; we are designed for real food. Here in Santa Barbara, California, the Orfalea Fund is working to create better food options in local schools. We've created the s'Cool Food initiative to bring better choices to cafeterias and better information about nutrition to students. The program seeks to create sustainable cooked-from-scratch food service systems and to procure as many school foods and beverages as practicable from providers near the school.

But the real goal is to improve the health and fitness of families, and to redeem the children's relationship with food so they can become healthy, productive adults.

I once invested a small amount in a very ambitious start-up company. The firm was started by a couple of fellows who made their fortunes with a high-tech Web company during the Internet stock market bubble of the 1990s. During our tour of their new facility, one of the company's managers showed us a small storeroom stocked to the ceiling with candy bars, soft drinks, microwaveable packaged meals, etc.

While I stared at the junk food temple, our tour guide confided with a grin that he expected his workers to pull a lot of all-nighters, so he rewarded them with these treats. Consciously or unconsciously, these entrepreneurs were using harmful, addictive substances to addict people to their work. I confess to smiling as I watched their stock price plummet over the coming months; it felt like karma.

If we are what we eat, let us choose to be fit, healthy, and smart. And let us choose to provide our coworkers with nutritious options that prove we care about them as human beings, not that we think of them as mere interchangeable parts.

Paul Orfalea

Questions:

1. What are the most nutritious foods available in your company's break room?
2. What connection might exist between your personal health-care costs and your diet?
3. When you read the nutrition label on the packaged food closest at hand, how many ingredients have names with more than four syllables? Hmmm.

Travel Is My Anti-Arrogance

I know a couple with a very common marital conflict: One of them likes to spend money to buy things, while the other spends money to do things. Even when they have enough money for both, it's a powerful conflict because of their competing philosophies: He values tangible possessions, while she values intangible experiences.

There are pros and cons to each point of view, but I'd much rather talk to her at a party. It's not just that she's far more attractive, although she is. It's that her stories are more interesting. He can tell you about the great deal he got on his latest gadget. She can tell you the comic tale of sitting in a café and watching three skinny, boisterous Italian men carry a giant flat-screen television into a Venetian apartment—from the tipsy boat to the steep, narrow, winding staircase to the angled door that would admit a television or a workman but not both ...

Experience makes her a compelling storyteller, and storytelling is a crucial entrepreneurial skill. In her preface to *Corporate Legends & Lore: The Power of Storytelling as a Management Tool* (PCN Associates, 1993), Peg Neuhauser writes:

> Storytelling has been used for thousands of years as a way of connecting the past, present, and future of a community's life. Without stories, it

> has always been difficult for people to know who
> they are or where they fit into a complex world
> around them ... Storytelling is the single most
> powerful form of human communication. It is
> the primary tool that human beings use to pass
> on their cultures. We can use it to inspire, teach,
> comfort, and entertain.

This applies to company culture as well, and that's why great business leaders tend to be great storytellers. Many mergers fail because when acquired, companies lose their experienced managers, then their stories, and eventually, their culture.

Traveling exposes us to many new stories and refills our well of experience in ways that books, movies, and television cannot. No matter where we go, traveling reminds us that all over the world and all over our own country, people live very differently and find unique solutions to common problems.

On recent travels to Africa and Spain, two first impressions were humbling and thought provoking. First, I met happy people everywhere I went. Regardless of conditions many in the United States would call poverty, it was clear to me that people in general, and children in particular, pursue happiness and often find it. You would not know this from watching television.

The second observation is undoubtedly connected to the first. Indigenous diets in many other countries are far healthier than the highly processed factory foods consumed in mass quantities in the United States of America. In much of the world, people eat locally grown, seasonal foods as a matter of course; here in the United States, such a bold act inspires best-selling books and local activist organizations. Remember that in the United States, obesity is the number-one health problem among the poor.

So my overall impression was that all else being equal—free of tyranny and communicable disease—people around the world seemed happier and healthier than my neighbors in allegedly wealthy Southern California. I'm a very proud American, but I'll be thinking about this for a while.

They say that travel broadens the mind. Wandering with open eyes brings education, humility, and appreciation for the diversity and ingenuity of mankind. Such perspective makes one a more empathetic leader, a better communicator, and a more resourceful problem solver. So, where are you going next?

Questions:

1. Reflecting on your last visit to another culture, what observations might provide lessons for your business?
2. What are the most repeated stories in your organization? Why?
3. When you travel, how does the experience compare to books, movies, and television shows about the place?

Sudden Silence

When the phones stopped ringing at the various trading rooms and offices of Lehman Brothers, what did the habitually overstimulated and hyperactive coworkers hear?

I mean, what did they hear after "I can't believe it" and "What do I do now?" had been uttered two or three times by each coworker? Later, as they sat in unnaturally quiet cubicles and offices, loading personal photos and coffee mugs into Bankers' Boxes□, could they hear their own breathing? Could they hear the rhythmic pulsing of their own hearts? Could they finally hear themselves think? If so, did they listen?

Many people today are addicted to constant activity—trained by television, video games, and a test-obsessed school system to resist idle moments or unstructured time. They are socially dependent, requiring the constant stimulation—and approval—of others. Some have been moving ninety miles per hour, 24/7 since elementary school, without a spare moment devoted to quiet self-reflection. Some found their dream jobs on Wall Street, where the action and the pressure never stop and self-doubt falls into the column labeled "liabilities."

When these type A individuals find themselves suddenly alone, are they equipped to reflect on their lives and actions so far? More to the point, are they psychologically prepared to deal with what they see in the mirror?

One of the biggest problems in our schools and workplaces is that we confuse activity with results, so we put a premium on busywork and busyness. But human beings need time for reflection because that is how we develop good judgment, and that is how we learn to live with ourselves.

There's a story about an American traveling in Africa. He hires a guide to lead him through the jungle to a remote village. In the afternoon, the guide stops to set up camp for the night. The American impatiently inquires why they aren't taking advantage of the remaining daylight to travel farther. "We have traveled very fast and must allow time for our souls to catch up with our bodies," says the guide.

A little quiet time, a little downtime, or even some pure fun dumb-time each day gives our souls a chance to catch up. Instead of preparing for the next test or meeting, we should be preparing for a greater test—how to live, how to think, how to be happy.

I sympathize with the workers at Lehman Brothers. When I left Kinko's after thirty years of constant activity, the silence was deafening. But I learned to appreciate the quiet. Able to hear myself think, I set about learning to listen better. And then I set about repurposing my life ...

Questions:

1. How much of each day do you devote to quiet self-reflection?

2. What is your position on unstructured time? Must you always be busy?

3. How do you know if you are doing the right thing? How do you know if you are happy?

Epilogue: Differences and Disabilities

I opened this book with a reflection on how my "disabilities" proved to be indispensable advantages in my life. Of course, I don't think of them as disabilities but rather as opportunities.

Although society's understanding of dyslexia and ADHD is improving, too many people still equate *difference* with *disability*. Every disability may be a difference, but not every difference is a disability. Children are sometimes branded *learning disabled*, even when it is their schools that actually lack ability. Schools that still treat education as a one-size-fits-all endeavor resent individualized instruction, which they consider inefficient. But our growing awareness of learning differences puts more enlightened schools in a difficult position: Within the constraints of budgets and teaching skills, how can we best serve students with differences?

What if we reframe the question? What if *every* student learns in a different way and at a different pace? That's right: What if everyone has a learning difference? Some may fit more neatly into traditional teaching templates, but does that make others *disabled*?

We hire specialists to identify and label disabilities, but we should be learning to recognize and support *hidden* abilities. Unfortunately, we've been moving in the opposite direction. Standardized testing, which is supposed to improve school accountability, actually makes schools accountable for the wrong outcomes. *Students of management learned long ago that we get what we measure. As currently executed, standardized testing measures the sameness of students, and uniformity is a dubious goal.*

Now reframe the question again: What if every workplace is in fact a school, and the company's success depends on each coworker's ability to learn and apply new ideas? How do we address each coworker's learning differences?

As I said in the introduction, you must be good at everything to succeed in school. But to be successful in life, you only have to be good at one or two things. I recognize the importance of a well-rounded education, but some people take a roundabout path to get there. For them, school should be a part of the journey paved with small victories, not an impassable mountain of accumulated failures and dismissive labels.

In the workplace, this equates to matching people's assignments with their skills and abilities, and developing their strengths to the limits of their ambition. For our businesses to keep growing, we must ensure that our coworkers keep growing.

Here's the biggest obstacle: Most hierarchical organizations embrace the false logic that efficiency improves results, consistency improves efficiency, and therefore, consistency improves results. But efficiency is a false idol. In most cases, the quest for efficiency serves the collective needs of managers and administrators more than it serves the unique needs of customers, constituents, or students. Organizations that prioritize results over process gladly trade some efficiency for greater effectiveness. What results do we expect from our students and coworkers?

Many of my Kinko's coworkers attended the Management Action Program, a workshop designed to help people build on their personal and professional strengths. Among other things, the workshop requires attendees to face a stark—and often harsh—appraisal of their professional strengths and weaknesses. But rather than dwell on weaknesses, as most people do, the program teaches attendees how to focus more attention on their strengths. Unless they are dangerous, weaknesses are to be ignored or marginalized.

Instead of obsessing over what a student or coworker cannot do, schools and workplaces should help each person make the most of his or her individual strengths because *you don't make a difference in this world by trying to be the same as everyone else.* That's true in business and in the pursuit of happiness.

These essays contain a lot of my thoughts on business and life, but the ultimate lesson of my experience is that one size does not fit all. *These reflections will be of real value if they inspire you to make your life and business more your own.* This is your life, your business, your day. Build of it what *you* will.

About the Authors

Paul Orfalea founded Kinko's in 1970 with a small loan cosigned by his father. Between 1970 and 2000, Paul, his partners, and coworkers built the company from a one-hundred-square-foot alcove into a $2 billion innovation factory with over one thousand locations. After leaving Kinko's, Paul co-founded West Coast Asset Management with Lance Helfert.

To support his philanthropic goals, Paul launched the Orfalea Family Foundation and the Orfalea Fund. Areas of focus for his philanthropy include:

- education and early care
- intergenerational programs
- learning differences and challenges
- critical community needs
- experiential enrichment.

Learn more about Paul at www.paulorfalea.com.

Dean Zatkowsky has worked with Paul Orfalea for more than twenty years, holding executive positions at three Orfalea-related companies: Kinko's, DataProse, and West Coast Asset Management. An operationally biased marketer, Dean believes that "to do better than the competition, you have to be better than the competition." In 2007, Dean founded Dizzy One Ventures LLC (www.dizzyone. net) to pursue personal writing projects, and to provide writing and publishing services.

www.ingramcontent.com/pod-product-compliance
Lightning Source LLC
Chambersburg PA
CBHW071226170526
45165CB00003B/1006